MEDITATIONS
OF
RALPH
WALDO
EMERSON

Into the
Green Future

D0166971

MEDITATIONS
OF
RALPH
WALDO
EMERSON

Into the
Green Future

Compiled and edited by
CHRIS HIGHLAND

 WILDERNESS PRESS · BERKELEY, CA

Meditations of Ralph Waldo Emerson: Into the Green Future

1st EDITION April 2004
  2nd printing April 2006
  3rd printing August 2008

Copyright © 2004 by Chris Highland

Foreword copyright © 2004 by Wesley T. Mott
Front cover and frontispiece portraits courtesy Joel Myerson
  Collection of Nineteenth-Century American
Literature, University of South Carolina
Other cover photos copyright © 2004 by Chris Highland
Interior photos, except where noted, by Chris Highland
Book and cover design by Larry B. Van Dyke

ISBN 978-0-89997-352-4
UPC 7-19609-97352-2

Manufactured in the United States of America

Published by: **Wilderness Press**
                1345 8th Street
                Berkeley, CA 94710
                (800) 443-7227; FAX (510) 558-1696
                info@wildernesspress.com
                www.wildernesspress.com

Visit our website for a complete listing of our books and for ordering information.

Cover photos: Emerson at age 51 (1854);
                  Glen Almond — Highlands, Scotland;
                  Fern fronds; Sunrise over Blue Ridge Mountains
                  — South Carolina
Frontispiece: Emerson at age 70 (1873)

To Sharel

Contents

Foreword

"A man is a method, a progressive arrangement; a selecting principle, gathering his like to him, wherever he goes."

~ Ralph Waldo Emerson
"Spiritual Laws"

The reputation of Ralph Waldo Emerson is as high as it has been since his death in 1882. As the national outpouring of editorials, magazine articles, lectures, conferences, and books during the 2003 bicentennial of Emerson's birth suggests, his appeal runs wide and deep, and around the globe he is regarded as representative of American culture.

Emerson's admirers frequently use terms such as "affirming" and "liberating" to describe his influence, and it is no coincidence that these are qualities Emerson himself ascribes to "the poet" in the essay of that name. Such terms came naturally to the "Sage of Concord," who had been a Unitarian minister at Second Church in Boston (1829–1832). Even though he resigned his position, he never formally resigned from the profession, serving as a supply preacher until 1839 and conceiving of his subsequent career as a lecturer as a natural transition from pulpit to lectern. But of course the sources of Emerson's own inspiration were famously eclectic — classical philosophy, Western religion, 18th century moral philosophy, European and British

Romanticism, and Eastern mysticism, not to mention all of the arts and even modern science.

It is not surprising that the Unitarians who once branded Emerson as a heretic have since embraced him as one of their own prophets. Nor is it surprising that so many modern readers look to Emerson as a spiritual—indeed as a religious—guide. Emerson's eminently quotable maxims (his "orphic" style) have made him especially appealing to readers seeking spiritual sustenance in an age when orthodox religion often fails to deliver. Some devotees of Emerson have even claimed to discern in his writings a "new Gospel" of truth.

The problem with such quests is that Emerson's own spirituality is extraordinarily varied and even surprising. He described himself as "an endless seeker," and having fought against the constraints and dogmatism of orthodoxy, he had no intention of establishing a *new* orthodoxy. Emerson is perhaps most famous for his ecstatic account of oneness with the universe—the wonderful "transparent eyeball" passage in "Nature" (1836). But he was also keenly aware that ecstasy cannot continually be sustained, wishing, in "The Transcendentalist," "to exchange this flash-of-lightning faith for continuous daylight." He admitted in "Experience" to being bedeviled by "the lords of life"—qualities of our own nature that thwart our attempts to understand— learning to be content with small victories after great struggle. Knowing that blinding conversions seldom occur, he grew to value most the "quotidian" truths—those of everyday life. And he came increasingly to insist that personal wisdom was nothing if not related to social justice, as he spoke out with growing intensity about the plight of Native Americans, slaves, and women in his society.

Emerson loved the timeless and the universal in truth—which is why, like all Transcendentalists, he felt his own daily life so connected to the utterances of writers and prophets from different ages and cultures. But he knew also that we *experience* truth on the run. Flux is the condition of nature, and "Man's life," he wrote in "Compensation," "is a progress, and not a station." Emerson thus refuses to offer comforting new creeds and easy assurance. But he does offer us an approach to wisdom, insisting in the same essay that "In the nature of the soul is the compensation for the inequalities of condition."

A truly Emersonian search for wisdom looks not for self-affirming external props of new doctrine but accepts insecurity and change as natural and human. Emerson warns us, in fact, that there is a certain fateful self-selecting quality to our quest. *We gather our like to ourselves wherever we go.* As a spiritual guide, Emerson gives us not so much comfort as "provocation," which he prescribes in the Divinity School Address. That is how Emerson still affirms and liberates us more than 200 years after his birth. That is the challenge awaiting you in this collection.

~ Wesley T. Mott
Worcester Polytechnic Institute
Past President, The Ralph Waldo Emerson Society

Introduction

"Emerson was the most serene, majestic,
sequoia-like soul I ever met." [1]

~ John Muir

I was first introduced to Ralph Waldo Emerson
(1803–1882) in a university course in Seattle. We
were reading early American "romantic" authors
including Thoreau, Whitman, Hawthorne, Poe and
Emerson. My imagination was enflamed by the
audacious freethinking of these early radicals.
Among his contemporaries Emerson stood out as
one who was unafraid of speaking his passionate
mind in pursuit of the frontiers of thought. He ford-
ed streams and bridged the wild places of the heart
and intellect in a way I had not seen in others.

When I first read Emerson I was emerging from a
fenced and packaged worldview of faith. I turned the
attention of my undergraduate studies to
Philosophy and its potential as a wise balance to
Religion. In Emerson I was exposed to a wisdom
that was incisive and competent in connecting honest religious sentiment with tough philosophical
inquiry. This was the beginning of my personal lib-
eration—a confluence of spirit and mind. I delighted to find someone who took seriously both
intellectual endeavor (asking the hard questions that
excite reasoning) and spiritual practice (living with
the hard questions that elicit meaning).

Born in Boston, Emerson was raised by his mother following the death of his father, a Unitarian minister. Throughout his time at Harvard College and Divinity School and during his brief service in the ordained ministry, he nurtured a spiritual philosophy that pushed past the edges of the popular beliefs of his day, and which would eventually develop into a movement he and his intellectual peers called "Transcendentalism." Diverging from the well-worn trail of his parents' tradition he discovered his own voice on a verdant path of enlightened insight expounded in lectures, essays and poems.

Tracing a footpath along the edges of mysticism he touched the overgrown border of Nature's intrinsic beauty. Speaking to young ministry students at Harvard he closed with these prophetic words: "I look for the hour when that supreme Beauty which ravished the souls of those Eastern men. . . shall speak in the West also"[2]. I am convinced that Emerson himself helped usher in that hour. Through his reflective explorations and his poetic, meditative thought Emerson articulates the Beauty that we all seek out beyond the boxed boundaries of preaching or politics. In this one early American thinker, East not only met West but embraced in a universal dance under the starry sky.

To those sauntering toward Beauty and Truth, Emerson offers a pause point, a hostel for pondering. His many essays reveal a person intrigued by the marginalized ideas that can reboot Life in all its wonder. In both his journals and written discourses I consistently find Emerson an apt guide for meditation. To the extent he is sought out for soul nourishment, Emerson will continue to provide inspiring guidance. A word of caution here. Emerson was a heretic. Heresy is choosing to walk another, often hazardous, path, discovering another way, branching

off from the "right opinions" of the orthodox guardians of traditional truth. The heretical way is open to the full array of options and choices; it fearlessly leaves known rivers to discover other streams, to climb higher toward peaks and perspectives perhaps never reached. The adventuring heretic is rarely welcomed or understood, but then, as Emerson reminds us, "To be great is to be misunderstood"[3]. Meditating with Emerson is as risky as slipping along a waterfall or sliding up a winding deerpath. Confidence comes from searching out the footfalls where, chances are, no one has gone before. Is there any greater way to exercise the human soul?

When I chose to leave my own tradition after 14 years as a Protestant minister, I could hear Emerson's voice like a wise owl in an old growth forest. I heard him say, "You are the Truth's and belong to no other"; "There are no other footprints but your own"; "Speak your truth today, though it contradict everything you said and believed yesterday." I sensed a parallel orbit with the wondering wanderer of Concord. Like him, I have come to find that Nature is, in Herself, the greatest spiritual teacher. Emerson too walked out of his parents' pulpit and religion, and it freed him to lecture, write, travel and develop fresh ideas-to kindle a fire and inspire. He explored and experimented with community and his own solitude. When I let go of the weeds of creeds, I knew, as I have innately known, that Emerson's wisdom is a well-watered, fertile field to be harvested for countless fruits. His crop is pragmatic and dynamically truthful, with the potential to empower our own emergence as free, mature, healthy and independent persons. He helped me leave the expected, acceptable path for higher passes and deeper lakes of vision. I have no regrets. And I keep meditating on his wisdom because it encourages me

to weave and widen my own unique greening philosophy of life.

In his journals Emerson muses, "The universe is a more amazing puzzle than ever" (quote 1). For the New England freethinker, the enigmatic art of Nature is brushed with hints of interconnection — an artistic web that mystifies even as it instructs. To muse with Emerson is to sense all things as bound together in a kind of fragile dreamcatcher. He sees no distant deity to ponder but a Oneness that permeates and continually communicates. In the selection entitled "Worship," our Chaplain of Creation offers this image: "The Supreme Being does not build up nature around us, but puts it forth through us, as the life of the tree puts forth new branches and leaves through the pores of the old" (quote 10). The natural world is a full expression of spirit and requires no mediation. The nature of things is to be united in a colorfully plural diversity — E Pluribus Unum. Though it seems we are never quite near enough to Nature's full countenance, it is within us to understand, to grasp that we share a common intimacy with the trees and all the stuff of the cosmos (quote 54). As Emerson's good friend Margaret Fuller wrote, "The earth is spirit made fruitful, — life."[4] We are intrinsically sustained by an indelible greenness.

If we invite him to be, Ralph Waldo Emerson can be a trusted companion for our spiritual pilgrimage. He can be for us, as he was for John Muir, a sequoia, solid symbol of serenity, heavy with seeds to catch. Like the stately sequoia, Emerson stands as a symbol of the ancient past and the potent promise of the future. His green future is now our green present and we have only to plant, nurture and grow, to flourish and to germinate, to assure our own, and Nature's, future. Use these selections from 30 years

of Emerson's writing to illumine—to light and delight—your way. Whatever the trail conditions, we can discover a guide in this pathfinder of the 19th century. Consider this collection, as I do, an essential survival item for your backpack. Carry Waldo, as his friends called him, into the landmarks of every land and he will remind that Nature is a parent, soulmate, and companion who shares familiar rivulets in the veins. This collection of wisdom will inspire your journeys into Nature's heart, pulsing along as a cool river toward a vigorous, vibrant, growing and green future.

~ Chris Highland
Winter 2004

1. John Muir. *John of the Mountains: The Unpublished Journals of John Muir.* Edited by Linnie Marsh Wolfe. Madison, Wisconsin: University of Wisconsin Press, 1966, p. 436.
2. "An Address." 1838. *The Complete Essays and Other Writings of Ralph Waldo Emerson.* N.Y.: The Modern Library, 1950, p. 84.
3. "Self-Reliance." 1841. Ibid., p. 152.
4. Margaret Fuller. "Summer on the Lakes." *The Portable Margaret Fuller.* Edited by Mary Kelley. N.Y.: Penguin Books, 1994, p. 78.

A Note on Inclusive Language

As a collector of wisdom, I feel Emerson must be heard today. We must let nothing block his message. Emerson stood as a herald of the 19th century's free and pioneering spirit. Unlike the timid person who "dares not say 'I think,' 'I am,' but quotes some saint or sage" ("Self-Reliance"), Emerson fearlessly explored new intellectual territory and challenged the old ways.

I call your attention to his use of terminology common in his era, especially his employment of male nouns and pronouns that can create awkward obstacles to a full understanding of his meanings. For us, to be "Man Thinking" it would surely be in Emerson's spirit to read "Humanity Thinking." When he says, "Man postpones or remembers; he does not live in the present," we can easily read "Humanity postpones or remembers; people do not live in the present." The same is true for references to the divine, where we could appropriately interchange Emerson's wonderful term "Oversoul." Simply substituting neutral or feminine words here and there can serve to deepen the spiritual significance of the essentially obsolete language, bringing wise words to life in our time.

This attention to interchange is especially urgent because of one clear fact: Emerson believed in the equality of women. In his *Journal* of October 14, 1851, he wrote, "I think that as long as [women] have not equal rights of property and right of voting they are not on the right footing." His friend and co-editor of *The Dial*, Margaret Fuller, who wrote *Woman*

in the Nineteenth Century, had a profound effect on Emerson. In her numerous letters to her "dear friend" whom she called "Waldo," this influential woman expressed equilibration in her own critiques and meditations. After her death in a shipwreck returning from Italy to New York in 1850, Emerson said his remarkable friend "was the largest woman, and not a woman who wanted to be a man."

In the following selections I have accurately quoted Emerson's own words. However, in honor of Margaret Fuller and her significant influence on Emerson the man, the thinker and the writer, I ask the reader to universalize the language of these meditations and to practice, in the present age, the fair and balanced art of "Humanity Thinking."

1

I Will Be a Naturalist

The universe is a more amazing puzzle than ever, as you glance along this bewildering series of animated forms, — the hazy butterflies, the carved shells, the birds, beasts, fishes, snakes, and the upheaving principle of life everywhere incipient, in the very rock aping organized forms. Not a form so grotesque, so savage, nor so beautiful but is an expression of some property inherent in man the observer, — an occult relation between the very scorpions and man. I feel the centipede in me, — cayman, carp, eagle, and fox. I am moved by strange sympathies; I say continually, "I will be a naturalist."

"Delight itself, however, is a weak term to express the feelings of a naturalist."

~ Charles Darwin
Voyage of the Beagle

2

The Noble Earth

Went yesterday to Cambridge and spent most of the day at Mount Auburn; got my luncheon at Fresh Pond, and went back again to the woods. After much wandering and seeing many things, four snakes gliding up and down a hollow for no purpose that I could see—not to eat, not for love, but only gliding; then a whole bed of *Hepatica triloba*, cousins of the Anemone, all blue and beautiful, but constrained by niggard nature to wear their last year's faded jacket of leaves; then a black-capped titmouse, who came upon a tree, and when I would know his name, sang *chick-a-dee-dee*; then a far-off tree full of clamourous birds, I know not what, but you might hear them half a mile; I forsook the tombs, and found a sunny hollow where the east wind would not blow, and lay down against the side of a tree to most happy beholdings. At least I opened my eyes and let what would pass through them into the soul. I saw no more my relation, how near and petty, to Cambridge or Boston; I heeded no more what minute or hour our Massachusetts clocks might indicate—I saw only the noble earth on which I was born, with the great Star which warms and enlightens it. I saw the clouds that hang their significant drapery over us. It was Day—that was all Heaven said. The pines glittered with their innumerable green needles in the light, and seemed to challenge me to read their riddle. The drab oak-leaves of the last year turned their little somersets and lay still again. And the wind bustled high overhead in the forest top. This gay and grand architecture, from the vault to the moss and lichen on which I lay, — who shall explain to me the laws of its proportions and adornments?

"In big wilderness [we leave tomorrow's men] a chance to seek answers to questions we have not yet learned how to ask."

~ David Brower
Gentle Wilderness

3

Mellow Beauty

No art can exceed the mellow beauty of one square rood of ground in the woods this afternoon. The noise of the locust, the bee, and the pine; the light, the insect forms, butterflies, cankerworms hanging, balloon-spiders swinging, devils-needles cruising, chirping grasshoppers; the tints and forms of the leaves and trees, — not a flower but its form seems a type, not a capsule but is an elegant seed-box, — then the myriad asters, polygalas, and golden-rods, and through the bush the far pines, and overhead the eternal sky. All the pleasing forms of art are imitations of these, and yet before the beauty of a right action all this beauty is cold and unaffecting.

"I have listened for a long time
to the silence
and gone deep into the wild grass."

~Anna Ione
"Into the Wild Grass," in *Intense and Joyful Blue*

4

Natural Relations

Cold, bright Sunday morn, white with deep snow. Charles thinks if a superior being should look into families, he would find natural relations existing, and man a worthy being, but if he followed them into shops, senates, churches, and societies, they would appear wholly artificial and worthless. Society seems noxious. I believe that against these baleful influences Nature is the antidote. The man comes out of the wrangle of the shop and office, and sees the sky and the woods, and is a man again. He not only quits the cabal, but he finds himself. But how few men see the sky and the woods!

"But it can also happen, if will and grace are joined, that as I contemplate the tree I am drawn into relation, and the tree ceases to be an It."

~ Martin Buber
I and Thou

5

Face to Face

Our age is retrospective. It builds the sepulchres of the fathers. It writes biographies, histories, and criticism. The foregoing generations beheld God and nature face to face; we, through their eyes. Why should not we also enjoy an original relation to the universe? Why should not we have a poetry and philosophy of insight and not of tradition, and a religion by revelation to us, and not the history of theirs? Embosomed for a season in nature, whose floods of life stream around and through us, and invite us, by the powers they supply, to action proportioned to nature, why should we grope among the dry bones of the past, or put the living generation into masquerade out of its faded wardrobe? The sun shines to-day also. There is more wool and flax in the fields. There are new lands, new men, new thoughts. Let us demand our own works and laws and worship.

*"Then arose in my breast a genuine admiration,
and a humble adoration of the Being
who was the architect of this and of all."*

~ Margaret Fuller
Summer on the Lakes

6

To Go Into Solitude

To go into solitude, a man needs to retire as much from his chamber as from society. I am not solitary whilst I read and write, though nobody is with me. But if a man would be alone, let him look at the stars. The rays that come from those heavenly worlds will separate between him and what he touches. One might think the atmosphere was made transparent with this design, to give man, in the heavenly bodies, the perpetual presence of the sublime. Seen in the streets of cities, how great they are! If the stars should appear one night in a thousand years, how would men believe and adore; and preserve for many generations the remembrance of the city of God which had been shown! But every night come out these envoys of beauty, and light the universe with their admonishing smile.

The stars awaken a certain reverence, because though always present they are inaccessible; but all natural objects make a kindred impression, when the mind is open to their influence. . . . Nature never became a toy to a wise spirit. The flowers, the animals, the mountains, reflected the wisdom of his best hour, as much as they had delighted the simplicity of his childhood.

"We need a quiet environment in order to undertake our practice. Most important, we need solitude."

~ The Dalai Lama
An Open Heart

7

On This Green Ball

The misery of man appears like childish petulance, when we explore the steady and prodigal provision that has been made for his support and delight on this green ball which floats him through the heavens. What angels invented these splendid ornaments, these rich conveniences, this ocean of air above, this ocean of water beneath, this firmament of earth between? this zodiac of lights, this tent of dropping clouds, this striped coat of climates, this fourfold year? Beasts, fire, water, stones, and corn serve him. The field is at once his floor, his work-yard, his play-ground, his garden, and his bed. . . .

Nature, in its ministry to man, is not only the material, but is also the process and the result. All the parts incessantly work into each other's hands for the profit of man. The wind sows the seed; the sun evaporates the sea; the wind blows the vapors to the field; the ice, on the other side of the planet, condenses rain on this; the rain feeds the plant; the plant feeds the animal; and thus the endless circulations of the divine charity nourish man.

"Thou didst create this earth to give us joy."

~ Zoroaster
Gathas

8

Follow Your Streams

Who looks upon a river in a meditative hour and is not reminded of the flux of all things? Throw a stone into the stream, and the circles that propagate themselves are the beautiful type of all influence. Man is conscious of a universal soul within or behind his individual life, wherein, as in a firmament, the natures of Justice, Truth, Love, Freedom, arise and shine. This universal soul he calls Reason: it is not mine, or thine, or his, but we are its; we are its property and men. And the blue sky in which the private earth is buried, the sky with its eternal calm, and full of everlasting orbs, is the type of Reason. That which intellectually considered we call Reason, considered in relation to nature, we call Spirit. Spirit is the Creator. Spirit hath life in itself. And man in all ages and countries embodies it in his language as the FATHER.

"This has God given to all creatures,
To foster and seek their own nature."

~ Mechthild of Magdeburg
in *Medieval Women Mystics*

9

My Beautiful Mother

I have no hostility to nature, but a child's love to it. I expand and live in the warm day like corn and melons. Let us speak her fair. I do not wish to fling stones at my beautiful mother, nor soil my gentle nest. I only wish to indicate the true position of nature in regard to man, wherein to establish man all right education tends; as the ground which to attain is the object of human life, that is, of man's connection with nature. . . .

Idealism sees the world in God. It beholds the whole circle of persons and things, of actions and events, of country and religion, not as painfully accumulated, atom after atom, act after act, in an aged creeping Past, but as one vast picture which God paints on the instant eternity for the contemplation of the soul.

"The earth is precious to the Great Spirit, and to harm the earth is to heap contempt on its Creator."

~ Chief Seattle
Letter to President Franklin Pierce, 1855

10

Worship

Through all its kingdoms, to the suburbs and out-
skirts of things, [Nature] is faithful to the cause
whence it had its origin. It always speaks of Spirit. It
suggests the absolute. It is a perpetual effect. It is a
great shadow pointing always to the sun behind us.

The aspect of Nature is devout. Like the figure of
Jesus, she stands with bended head, and hands fold-
ed upon the breast. The happiest man is the one
who learns from nature the lesson of worship.

Of that ineffable essence which we call Spirit, he
that thinks most, will say least. We can foresee God
in the coarse, and, as it were, distant phenomena of
matter; but when we try to define and describe himself, both language and thought desert us, and we
are as helpless as fools and savages. That essence
refuses to be recorded in propositions, but when
man has worshipped him intellectually, the noblest
ministry of nature is to stand as the apparition of
God. . . .

Therefore, that spirit, that is, the Supreme Being,
does not build up nature around us, but puts it
forth through us, as the life of the tree puts forth
new branches and leaves through the pores of the

old. As a plant upon the earth, so a man rests upon the bosom of God; he is nourished by unfailing fountains, and draws at his need inexhaustible power.

"You might step on a stone and it would be a more pious act."

~ Meister Eckhart
in *Classics of Western Spirituality*

11

By Your Hands

It will not need, when the mind is prepared for study, to search for objects. The invariable mark of wisdom is to see the miraculous in the common. What is a day? What is a year? What is summer? What is woman? What is a child? What is sleep? To our blindness, these things seem unaffecting. We make fables to hide the baldness of the fact and conform it, as we say, to the higher law of the mind. But when the fact is seen under the light of an idea, the gaudy fable fades and shrivels. We behold the real higher law. To the wise, therefore, a fact is true poetry, and the most beautiful of fables. These wonders are brought to our own door. You also are a man. Man and woman and their social life, poverty, labor, sleep, fear, fortune, are known to you. Learn that none of these things is superficial, but that each phenomenon has its roots in the faculties and affections of the mind. Whilst the abstract question occupies your intellect, nature brings it in the concrete to be solved by your hands. It were a wise inquiry for the closet, to compare, point by point, especially at remarkable crises in life, our daily history with the rise and progress of ideas in the mind.

So shall we come to look at the world with new eyes. . . .

Every spirit builds itself a house, and beyond its house a world, and beyond its world a heaven. Know then that the world exists for you. . . . Build therefore your own world.

"Dear Lord, I will remain restless, tense, and dissatisfied until I can be totally at peace in your house."

~ Henri Nouwen
quoted in *All Saints*

12

The Secret of Nature

"Miracles have ceased." Have they indeed? When? They had not ceased this afternoon when I walked into the wood and got into bright, miraculous sunshine, in shelter from the roaring wind. Who sees a pine-cone, or the turpentine exuding from the tree, or a leaf, the unit of vegetation, fall from its bough, as if it said, "the year is finished," or hears in the quiet, piny glen the chickadee chirping his cheerful note, or walks along the lofty promontory-like ridges which, like natural causeways, traverse the morass, or gazes upward at the rushing clouds, or downward at a moss or a stone and says to himself, "Miracles have ceased"?. . . .

Tell me where is the manufactory of this air, so thin, so blue, so restless, which eddies around you, in which your life floats, of which your lungs are but an organ, and which you coin into musical words. I am agitated with curiosity to know the secret of nature. Why cannot geology, why cannot botany speak and tell me what has been, what is, as I run along the forest promontory, and ask when it rose like a blister on heated steel? Then I looked up and saw the sun shining in the vast sky, and heard the wind bellow above and the water glistened in the vale. These were the forces that wrought then and work now. Yes, there they grandly speak to all plainly, in proportion as we are quick to apprehend.

"All the way to heaven is heaven."

~Catherine of Siena
in *Classics of Western Spirituality*

13

Humanity Thinking

Man is not a farmer, or a professor, or an engineer, but he is all. Man is priest, and scholar, and statesman, and producer, and soldier. . . . The state of society is one in which the members have suffered amputation from the trunk, and strut about so many walking monsters—a good finger, a neck, a stomach, an elbow, but never a man.

Man is thus metamorphosed into a thing, into many things. The planter, who is Man sent out into the field to gather food, is seldom cheered by any idea of the true dignity of his ministry. He sees his bushel and his cart, and nothing beyond, and sinks into the farmer, instead of Man on the farm. The tradesman scarcely ever gives an ideal worth to his work, but is ridden by the routine of his craft, and the soul is subject to dollars. The priest becomes a form; the attorney a statute-book; the mechanic a machine; the sailor a rope of the ship.

In this distribution of functions the scholar is the delegated intellect. In the right state he is Man Thinking. . . .

Him Nature solicits with all her placid, all her monitory pictures; him the past instructs; him the future invites.

"A branch cut off from the adjacent branch must of necessity be cut off from the whole tree also."

~ Marcus Aurelius
Meditations

14

This Web of God

The first in time and the first in importance of the influences upon the mind is that of nature. Every day, the sun; and, after sunset, Night and her stars. Ever the winds blow; ever the grass grows. Every day, men and women, conversing—beholding and beholden. The scholar is he of all men whom this spectacle most engages. He must settle its value in his mind. What is nature to him? There is never a beginning, there is never an end, to the inexplicable continuity of this web of God, but always circular power returning into itself. Therein it resembles his own spirit, whose beginning, whose ending, he never can find—so entire, so boundless.

"Heaven's net casts wide."

~ The Tao
Seventy-three

15

From One Root

Thus to him, to this schoolboy under the bending dome of day, is suggested that he and it proceed from one root; one is leaf and one is flower; relation, sympathy, stirring in every vein. And what is that root? Is not that the soul of his soul? A thought too bold; a dream too wild. Yet when this spiritual light shall have revealed the law of more earthly natures —when he has learned to worship the soul, and to see that the natural philosophy that now is, is only the first gropings of its gigantic hand, he shall look forward to an ever expanding knowledge as to a becoming creator. He shall see that nature is the opposite of the soul, answering to it part for part. One is seal and one is print. Its beauty is the beauty of his own mind. Its laws are the laws of his own mind. Nature then becomes to him the measure of his attainments. So much of nature as he is ignorant of, so much of his own mind does he not yet possess. And, in fine, the ancient precept, "Know thyself," and the modern precept, "Study nature," become at last one maxim.

"*Then by a sunne-beam
I will climbe to thee.*"

~ George Herbert
Poems

16

Currents of Warm Life

If there is any period one would desire to be born in, is it not the age of Revolution; when the old and the new stand side by side and admit of being compared; when the energies of all men are searched by fear and by hope; when the historic glories of the old can be compensated by the rich possibilities of the new era? This time, like all times, is a very good one, if we but know what to do with it.

I read with some joy of the auspicious signs of the coming days, as they glimmer already through poetry and art, through philosophy and science, through church and state.

One of these signs is the fact that the same movement which effected the elevation of what was called the lowest class in the state, assumed in literature a very marked and as benign an aspect. Instead of the sublime and beautiful, the near, the low, the common, was explored and poetized. That which had been negligently trodden under foot by those who were harnessing and provisioning themselves for long journeys into far countries, is suddenly found to be richer than all foreign parts. The literature of the poor, the feelings of the child, the philosophy of the street, the meaning of household life, are the topics of the time. It is a great stride. It is a sign—is it not?—of new vigor when the extremities are made active, when currents of warm life run into the hands and the feet. . . . I embrace the common, I explore and sit at the feet of the familiar, the low. . . . Show me the sublime presence of the highest spiritual cause lurking, as always it does lurk, in these suburbs and extremities of nature.

"May my blood be the seed of liberty."

~ Archbishop Oscar Romero
quoted in *All Saints*

17

World Enough for Us

Yesterday afternoon I went to the Cliff with Henry Thoreau. Warm, pleasant, misty weather, which the great mountain amphitheatre seemed to drink in with gladness. A crow's voice filled all the miles of air with sound. A bird's voice, even a piping frog, enlivens a solitude and makes world enough for us. At night I went out into the dark and saw a glimmering star and heard a frog, and Nature seemed to say, Well do not these suffice? Here is a new scene, a new experience. Ponder it, Emerson, and not like the foolish world, hanker after thunders and multitudes and vast landscapes, the sea or Niagara.

"Nothing is far from God."

~ St. Monica
in the *Confessions of Augustine*

18

The Wild Apple Bloomed God

In the wood, God was manifest, as God was not in the sermon. In the cathedralled larches the ground-pine crept God, the thrush sung God, the robin complained God, the cat-bird mewed God, the anemone vibrated God, the wild apple bloomed God; the ants built their little Timbuctoo wide abroad; the wild grape budded; the rye was in the blade; high overhead, high over cloud, the faint, sharp-horned moon sailed steadily west through fleets of little clouds; the sheaves of the birch brightened into green below. The pines kneaded their aromatics in the sun.

*"The trees and grasses were not withered any more
and murmured happily together,
and every living being cried in gladness
with whatever voice it had."*

~ Black Elk
Black Elk Speaks

19

Into the Green Future

I went at sundown to the top of [stepgrandfather] Dr. Ripley's hill and renewed my vows to the Genius of that place. Somewhat of awe, somewhat grand and solemn mingles with the beauty that shines afar around. In the West, where the sun was sinking behind clouds, one pit of splendour lay as in a desert of space, —a deposit of *still light*, not radiant. Then I beheld the river, like God's love, journeying out of the grey past on into the green future.

"I love to see and sit on rocks which I have known,
and pry into their moss, and see unchangeableness so established.
I not yet gray on rocks forever gray,
I no longer green under the evergreens."

~ Henry David Thoreau
A Week on the Concord and Merrimack Rivers

20

Breath of Life

In this refulgent summer, it has been a luxury to draw the breath of life. The grass grows, the buds burst, the meadow is spotted with fire and gold in the tint of flowers. The air is full of birds, and sweet with the breath of the pine, the balm-of-Gilead, and the new hay. Night brings no gloom to the heart with its welcome shade. Through the transparent darkness the stars pour their almost spiritual rays. Man under them seems a young child, and his huge globe a toy. The cool night bathes the world as with a river, and prepares his eyes again for the crimson dawn. The mystery of nature was never displayed more happily. The corn and the wine have been freely dealt to all creatures, and the never-broken silence with which the old bounty goes forward has not yielded yet one word of explanation. One is constrained to respect the perfection of this world in which our senses converse. How wide; how rich; what invitation from every property it gives to every faculty of man! In its fruitful soils; in its navigable sea; in its mountains of metal and stone; in its forests of all woods; in its animals; in its chemical ingredients; in the powers and path of light, heart, attraction and life, it is well worth the pith and heart of great men to subdue and enjoy it. . . .

What am I? and What is? asks the human spirit with a curiosity new-kindled, but never to be quenched. . . . Behold these infinite relations, so like, so unlike; many, yet one.

"Allowing nature to take over proved easier than I imagined."

~ David Masumoto
Epitaph for a Peach

21

Religion of Joy

The perception of this law of laws awakens in the mind a sentiment which we call the religious sentiment, and which makes our highest happiness. Wonderful is its power to charm and to command. It is a mountain air. It is the embalmer of the world. It is myrrh and storax, and chlorine and rosemary. It makes the sky and the hills sublime, and the silent song of the stars is it. By it is the universe made safe and habitable, not by science or power. Thought may work cold and intransitive in things, and find no end or unity; but the dawn of the sentiment of virtue on the heart, gives and is the assurance that Law is sovereign over all natures; and the worlds, time, space, eternity, do seem to break out into joy.

This sentiment is divine and deifying. It is the beatitude of man.

"Toughmindedness without tenderheartedness is cold and detached, leaving one's life in perpetual winter devoid of the warmth of spring and the gentle heat of summer."

~ Martin Luther King, Jr.
The Strength to Love

22

My Garden is Nearer

I know no means of calming the fret and perturbation into which too much sitting, too much talking, brings me, so perfect as labor. I have no animal spirits; therefore, when surprised by company and kept in a chair for many hours, my heart sinks, my brow is clouded and I think I will run for Acton woods, and live with the squirrels henceforward. But my garden is nearer, and my good hoe, as it bites the ground, revenges my wrongs, and I have less lust to bite my enemies. I confess I work at first with a little venom, lay to a little unnecessary strength. But by smoothing the rough hillocks, I smooth my temper; by extracting the long roots of the piper-grass, I draw out my own splinters; and in a short time I can hear the bobolink's song and see the blessed deluge of light and colour that rolls around me.

"To season one's destiny with the dust of one's folly, that is the trick."

~ Henry Miller
Big Sur

23

I Can Hardly Believe It Exists

We walked this afternoon to Edmund Hosmer's and Walden Pond. The South wind blew and filled with bland and warm light the dry sunny woods. The last year's leaves flew like birds through the air. As I sat on the bank of the Drop, or God's Pond, and saw the amplitude of the little water, what space, what verge, the little scudding fleets of ripples found to scatter and spread from side to side and take so much time to cross the pond, and saw how the water seemed made for the wind, and the wind for the water, dear playfellows for each other, —I said to my companion, I declare this world is so beautiful that I can hardly believe it exists.

*"I thought that these brief glimpses of nature's beauty
are also gifts of a kind, blessings from a world outside ourselves
to the world within."*

~ Tim McNulty
The Art of Nature

24

In the Presence of Nature

I went into the woods. I found myself not wholly present there. If I looked at a pine-tree or an aster, *that* did not seem to be Nature. Nature was still elsewhere: this, or this was but outskirt and far-off reflection and echo of the triumph that had passed by and was now as its glancing splendor and hey-day, — perchance in the neighboring fields, or, if I stood in the field, then in the adjacent woods. Always the present object gave me this sense of the stillness that follows a pageant that has just gone by.

"Wisdom is the true believer's stray camel."

~ Rumi
Selected Writings

25

Where One Ray Should Fall

There is a time in every man's education when he arrives at the conviction that envy is ignorance; that imitation is suicide; that he must take himself for better for worse as his portion; that though the wide universe is full of good, no kernel of nourishing corn can come to him but through his toil bestowed on that plot of ground which is given to him to till. The power which resides in him is new in nature, and none but he knows what that is which he can do, nor does he know until he has tried. Not for nothing one face, one character, one fact, makes much impression on him, and another none. This sculpture in the memory is not without preestablished harmony. The eye was placed where one ray should fall, that it might testify of that particular ray. We but half express ourselves, and are ashamed of that divine idea which each of us represents. It may be safely trusted as proportionate and of good issues, so it be faithfully imparted, but God will not have his work made manifest by cowards. A man is relieved and gay when he has put his heart into his work and done his best; but what he has said or done otherwise shall give him no peace. It is a deliverance which does not deliver. In the attempt his genius deserts him; no muse befriends; no invention, no hope.

Trust thyself: every heart vibrates to that iron string.

*"A fiery light kindled all my heart. . .,
just as the sun warms anything on which its rays fall."*

~ Hildegard of Bingen
Mystical Writings

26

Wood-life

I suppose no man can violate his nature. All the sallies of his will are rounded in by the law of his being, as the inequalities of Andes and Himmaleh are insignificant in the curve of the sphere. Nor does it matter how you gauge and try him. A character is like an acrostic or Alexandrian stanza; read it forward, backward, or across, it still spells the same thing. In this pleasing contrite wood-life which God allows me, let me record day by day my honest thought without prospect or retrospect, and, I cannot doubt, it will be found symmetrical, though I mean it not and see it not. My book should smell of pines and resound with the hum of insects. The swallow over my window should interweave that thread or straw he carries in his bill into my web also. We pass for what we are. Character teaches above our wills. Men imagine that they communicate their virtue or vice only by overt actions, and do not see that virtue or vice emit a breath every moment.

There will be an agreement in whatever variety of actions, so they be each honest and natural in their hour.

"Nothing would give up life:
Even the dirt kept breathing a small breath."

~ Theodore Roethke
"Root Cellar"

27

All Things Are Made Sacred

The relations of the soul to the divine spirit are so pure that it is profane to seek to interpose helps. It must be that when God speaketh he should communicate, not one thing, but all things; should fill the world with his voice; should scatter forth light, nature, time, souls, from the centre of the present thought; and new date and new create the whole. Whenever a mind is simple and receives a divine wisdom, old things pass away—means, teachers, texts, temples fall; it lives now, and absorbs past and future into the present hour. All things are made sacred by relation to it—one as much as another. All things are dissolved to their centre by their cause, and in the universal miracle petty and particular miracles disappear. If therefore a man claims to know and speak of God and carries you backward to the phraseology of some old mouldered nation in another country, in another world, believe him not.

Is the acorn better than the oak which is its fullness and completion?

"I am content to learn from [followers of other paths]
and to walk with them side by side toward the God who lives,
I believe, beyond the images that bind and blind us all."

~ John Shelby Spong
The Bishop's Voice

28

Roses Are Roses

Man is timid and apologetic; he is no longer upright; he dares not say "I think," "I am," but quotes some saint or sage. He is ashamed before the blade of grass or the blowing rose. These roses under my window make no reference to former roses or to better ones; they are for what they are; they exist with God today. There is no time to them. There is simply the rose; it is perfect in every moment of its existence. Before a leaf-bud has burst, its whole life acts; in the full-blown flower there is no more; in the leafless root there is no less. Its nature is satisfied and it satisfies nature in all moments alike. But man postpones or remembers; he does not live in the present, but with reverted eye laments the past, or, heedless of the riches that surround him, stands on tiptoe to foresee the future. He cannot be happy and strong until he too lives with nature in the present, above time.

"Life consists of rare, isolated moments of the greatest significance."

~ Friedrich Nietzsche
Human, All Too Human

29

No Other Footprints

When a man lives with God, his voice shall be as sweet as the murmur of the brook and the rustle of the corn.

And now at last the highest truth on this subject remains unsaid; probably cannot be said; for all that we say is the far-off remembering of the intuition. That thought by what I can now nearest approach to say it, is this. When good is near you, when you have life in yourself, it is not by any known or accustomed way; you shall not discern the foot-prints of any other; you shall not see the face of man; you shall not hear any name; the way, the thought, the good, shall be wholly strange and new. It shall exclude example and experience. You take the way from man, not to man. All persons that ever existed are its forgotten ministers. Fear and hope are alike beneath it. There is somewhat low even in hope. In the hour of vision there is nothing that can be called gratitude, nor properly joy. . . .

Vast spaces of nature, the Atlantic Ocean, the South Sea; long intervals of time, years, centuries, are of no account. This which I think and feel

underlay every former state of life and circum-
stances, as it does underlie my present, and what is
called life and what is called death.

Life only avails, not the having lived.

"The Earth, its life am I,
The sky, its life am I—
The mountains, its life am I—
The Sun, its life am I—
White corn, its life am I—
Yellow corn, its life am I—
The corn beetle, its life am I."

~ Navaho
from *The Essential Mystics*

30

To Beg a Cup of Water

The genesis and maturation of a planet, its poise and orbit, the bended tree recovering itself from the strong wind, the vital resources of every animal and vegetable, are demonstrations of the self-sufficing and therefore self-relying soul.

Thus all concentrates: let us not rove; let us sit at home with the cause. Let us stun and astonish the intruding rabble of men and books and institutions by a simple declaration of the divine fact. Bid the invaders take the shoes from off their feet, for God is here within. Let our simplicity judge them, and our docility to our own law demonstrate the poverty of nature and fortune beside our native riches.

But now we are a mob. Man does not stand in awe of man, nor is his genius admonished to stay at home, to put itself in communication with the internal ocean, but it goes abroad to beg a cup of water of the urns of other men. We must go alone.

"I will make the whole earth my altar."

~ Pierre Teilhard de Chardin
"The Mass on the World"

31

Higher Prayer

Prayer looks abroad and asks for some foreign addition to come through some foreign virtue, and loses itself in endless mazes of natural and supernatural, and mediatorial and miraculous. Prayer that craves a particular commodity, anything less than all good, is vicious. Prayer is the contemplation of the facts of life from the highest point of view. It is the soliloquy of a beholding and jubilant soul. It is the spirit of God pronouncing his works good. But prayer as a means to effect a private end is meanness and theft. It supposes dualism and not unity in nature and consciousness. As soon as the man is at one with God, he will not beg. He will then see prayer in all action. The prayer of the farmer kneeling in his field to weed it, the prayer of the rower kneeling with the stroke of his oar, are true prayers heard throughout nature, though for cheap ends.

Everywhere I am hindered of meeting God in my brother, because he has shut his own temple doors and recites fables merely of his brother's, or his brother's brother's God.

"*I intended to pray, too, as my only activity, pray for all living creatures; I saw it was the only decent activity left in the world.*"

~ Jack Kerouac
The Dharma Bums

32

My Giant

Travelling is a fool's paradise. Our first journeys discover to us the indifference of places. At home I dream that at Naples, at Rome, I can be intoxicated with beauty and lose my sadness. I pack my trunk, embrace my friends, embark on the sea and at last wake up in Naples, and there beside me is the stern fact, the sad self, unrelenting, identical, that I fled from. I seek the Vatican and the palaces. I affect to be intoxicated with sights and suggestions, but I am not intoxicated. My giant goes with me wherever I go.

But the rage of travelling is a symptom of a deeper unsoundness affecting the whole intellectual action. The intellect is vagabond, and our system of education fosters restlessness. Our minds travel when our bodies are forced to stay at home. We imitate; and what is imitation but the travelling of the mind?. . . .

Insist on yourself; never imitate. Your own gift you can present every moment with the cumulative force of a whole life's cultivation; but of the adopted talent of another you have only an extemporaneous half possession. That which each can do best, none but his Maker can teach him.

*"The heart has to learn suffering
or it will never be able to sing about it."*

~ Hans Christian Andersen
"The Old Church Bell"

33

Path from the Heart

When I look at the sweeping sleet amid the pine woods, my sentences look very contemptible, and I think I will never write more: but the words prompted by an irresistible charity, the words whose path from the heart to the lips I cannot follow, — are fairer than the snow. It is pitiful to be an artist. . . .

All my thoughts are foresters. I have scarce a day-dream on which the breath of the pines has not blown, and their shadows waved. Shall I not then call my little book Forest Essays?

"The mind can go in a thousand directions,
but on this beautiful path, I walk in peace.
With each step, a cool wind blows.
With each step, a flower blooms."

~ Thich Nhat Hanh
Stepping into Freedom

34

Lowly Listening

A little consideration of what takes place around us every day would show us that a higher law than that of our will regulates events; that our painful labors are unnecessary and fruitless; that only in our easy, simple, spontaneous action are we strong, and by contenting ourselves with obedience we become divine. Belief and love — a believing love will relieve us of a vast load of care. O my brothers, God exists. There is a soul at the centre of nature and over the will of every man, so that none of us can wrong the universe. It has so infused its strong enchantment into nature that we prosper when we accept its advice, and when we struggle to wound its creatures our hands are glued to our sides, or they beat our own breasts. The whole course of things goes to teach us faith. We need only obey. There is guidance for each of us, and by lowly listening we shall hear the right word. . . .

Place yourself in the middle of the stream of power and wisdom which animates all whom it floats, and you are without effort impelled to truth, to right and a perfect contentment.

*"In the eyes of God, the infinite spirit,
all the millions that have lived and now live
do not make a crowd;
God only sees each individual."*

~ Søren Kierkegaard
The Diary

35

The Passion

The passion rebuilds the world for the youth. It makes all things alive and significant. Nature grows conscious. Every bird on the boughs of the tree sings now to his heart and soul. The notes are almost articulate. The clouds have faces as he looks on them. The trees of the forest, the waving grass and the peeping flowers have grown intelligent; and he almost fears to trust them with the secret which they seem to invite. Yet nature soothes and sympathizes. In the green solitude he finds a dearer home than with men. . . .

Behold there in the wood the fine madman! He is a palace of sweet sounds and sights; he dilates; he is twice a man; he walks with arms akimbo; he soliloquizes; he accosts the grass and the trees; he feels the blood of the violet, the clover and the lily in his veins; and he talks with the brook that wets his foot.

*"This Soul is engraved in God,
and has her true imprint maintained
through the union of Love."*

~ Marguerite Porete
Mirror of Simple Souls

36

Shelter

I do not wish to treat friendships daintily, but with roughest courage. When they are real, they are not glass threads or frost-work, but the solidst thing we know. For now, after so many ages of experience, what do we know of nature or of ourselves? Not one step has man taken toward the solution of the problem of his destiny. In one condemnation of folly stand the whole universe of men. But the sweet sincerity of joy and peace which I draw from this alliance with my brother's soul is the nut itself whereof all nature and all thought is but the husk and shell. Happy is the house that shelters a friend!. . .

There are two elements that go to the composition of friendship, each so sovereign that I can detect no superiority in either, no reason why either should be first named. One is truth. A friend is a person with whom I may be sincere. Before him I may think aloud. . . . Every man alone is sincere. At the entrance of a second person, hypocrisy begins. . . .

The other element of friendship is tenderness. . . . Can another be so blessed and we so pure that we can offer him tenderness? When a man becomes dear to me I have touched the goal of fortune. . . .

It is fit for serene days and graceful gifts and country rambles, but also for rough roads and hard fare, shipwreck, poverty and persecution. It keeps company with the sallies of the wit and the trances of religion. We are to dignify to each other the daily needs and offices of man's life, and embellish it by courage, wisdom and unity.

"Homelessness, not only just for a shelter made of stone, but that homelessness that comes from having no one to call your own."

~ Mother Teresa of Calcutta
My Life for the Poor

37

We Are a Stream

Man is a stream whose source is hidden. Our being is descending into us from we know not whence. . . .

When I watch that flowing river, which, out of regions I see not, pours for a season its streams into me, I see that I am a pensioner; not a cause but a surprised spectator of this ethereal water; that I desire and look up and put myself in the attitude of reception, but from some alien energy the visions come.

The Supreme Critic on the errors of the past and the present, and the only prophet of that which must be, is that great nature in which we rest as the earth lies in the soft arms of the atmosphere; that Unity, that Over-Soul, within which every man's particular being is contained and made one with all other; that common heart of which all sincere conversation is the worship, to which all right action is submission; that over-powering reality which confutes our tricks and talents, and constrains every one to pass for what he is, and to speak from his character and not from his tongue, and which evermore tends to pass into our thought and hand and become wisdom and virtue and power and beauty.

We live in succession, in division, in parts, in particles. Meantime within man is the soul of the whole;
the wise silence; the universal beauty, to which
every part and particle is equally related; the eternal
ONE.

"And lo, my brook became a river,
and my river became a sea."

~ Sirach
Twenty-four
The Essential Mystics

38

Without a Bell

All reform aims in some one particular to let the soul have its way through us; in other words, to engage us to obey.

Of this pure nature every man is at some time sensible. Language cannot paint it with his colors. It is too subtile. It is undefinable, unmeasurable; but we know that it pervades and contains us. We know that all spiritual being is in man. A wise old proverb says, "God comes to see us without bell;" that is, as there is no screen or ceiling between our heads and the infinite heavens, so is there no bar or wall in the soul, where man, the effect, ceases, and God, the cause, begins. The walls are taken away. We lie open on one side to the deeps of spiritual nature, to the attributes of God. Justice we see and know, Love, Freedom, Power. These natures no man ever got above, but they tower over us, and most in the moment when our interests tempt us to wound them. . . . The soul circumscribes all things. . . .

The soul looketh steadily forwards, creating a world before her, leaving worlds behind her. She has no dates, nor rites, nor persons, nor specialties, nor men. The soul knows only the soul; the web of events is the flowing robe in which she is clothed.

"In Brahman are woven the sky and the earth
and all the regions of the air,
and in Brahman rest the mind and all the powers of life."

~ Mundaka Upanishad
The Upanishads, Mascaro translation

39

By the Same Fire

It is not in an arbitrary "decree of God," but in the nature of man, that a veil shuts down on the facts of tomorrow; for the soul will not have us read any other cipher than that of cause and effect. By this veil which curtains events it instructs the children of men to live in today. The only mode of obtaining an answer to these questions of the senses is to forego all low curiosity, and, accepting the tide of being which floats us into the secret of nature, work and live, work and live, and all unawares the advancing soul has built and forged for itself a new condition, and the question and the answer are one.

By the same fire, vital, consecrating, celestial, which burns until it shall dissolve all things into waves and surges of an ocean of light, we see and know each other, and what spirit each is of. . . .

If a man has not found his home in God, his manners, his forms of speech, the turn of his sentences, the build, shall I say, of all his opinions will involuntarily confess it, let him brave it out how he will. If we have found his centre, the Deity will shine through him, through all the disguises of ignorance, of ungenial temperament, of unfavorable circumstance. The tone of seeking is one, and the tone of having is another.

But genius is religious. It is a larger imbibing of the common heart.

"There may be a great fire in our soul. . .
Must one tend that inward fire?"

~ Vincent van Gogh
Letter to Theo

40

The Heart of All

When we have broken our god of tradition and ceased from our god of rhetoric, then may God fire the heart with his presence. It is the doubling of the heart itself, nay, the infinite enlargement of the heart with a power of growth to a new infinity on every side. It inspires in man an infallible trust. . . . O, believe, as thou livest, that every sound that is spoken over the round world, which thou oughtest to hear, will vibrate on thine ear! Every proverb, every book, every byword that belongs to thee for aid or comfort, shall surely come home through open or winding passages. Every friend whom not thy fantastic will but the great and tender heart in thee craveth, shall lock thee in his embrace. And this because the heart in thee is the heart of all; not a valve, not a wall, not an intersection is there anywhere in nature, but one blood rolls uninterruptedly an endless circulation through all men, as the water of the globe is all one sea, and, truly seen, its tide is one.

"Look into my heart!
There you will learn what my teacher is."

~Yehudah Zevi
in *Tales of the Hasidim*

41

Circle Within Circle

The eye is the first circle; the horizon which it forms is the second; and throughout nature this primary figure is repeated without end. It is the highest emblem in the cipher of the world. St. Augustine described the nature of God as a circle whose centre was everywhere and its circumference nowhere. We are all our lifetime reading the copious sense of this first of forms. One moral we have already deduced in considering the circular or compensatory character of every human action. Another analogy we shall now trace, that every action admits of being outdone. Our life is an apprenticeship to the truth that around every circle another can be drawn; that there is no end in nature, but every end is a beginning; that there is always another dawn risen on mid-noon, and under every deep a lower deep opens. . . .

Nature looks provokingly stable and secular, but it has a cause like all the rest; and when once I comprehend that, will these fields stretch so immovably wide, these leaves hang so individually considerable? Permanence is a word of degrees. Every thing is medial. Moons are no more bounds to spiritual power than bat-balls. . . .

The life of man is a self-evolving circle, which, from a ring imperceptibly small, rushes on all sides outwards to new and larger circles, and that without end. The extent to which this generation of circles, wheel without wheel, will go, depends on the force or truth of the individual soul.

"Thus a person finds that the God whom he was searching for over hill and dale, whom he was seeking in every brook, in every temple, in churches and heavens, that God is his own Self."

~ Vivekananda
What Religion Is

42

Immersed in Beauty

We are immersed in beauty, but our eyes have no clear vision. It needs, by the exhibition of single traits, to assist and lead the dormant taste. We carve and paint, or we behold what is carved and painted, as students of the mystery of Form. . . .

For every object has its roots in central nature, and may of course be so exhibited to us as to represent the world. Therefore each work of genius is the tyrant of the hour and concentrates attention on itself. For the time, it is the only thing worth naming to do that—be it a sonnet, an opera, a landscape, a statue, an oration, the plan of a temple, or a campaign, or of a voyage of discovery. Presently we pass to some other object, which rounds itself into a whole as did the first; for example a well-laid garden; and nothing seems worth doing but the laying out of gardens. I should think fire the best thing in the world, if I were not acquainted with air, and water, and earth. . . .

If the artist can draw every thing, why draw any thing? and then is my eye opened to the eternal picture which nature paints in the street, with moving men and children, beggars and fine ladies, draped in red and green and blue and gray; long-haired, grizzled, white-faced, black-faced, wrinkled, giant, dwarf, expanded, elfish—capped and based by heaven, earth and sea. . . .

Though we travel the world over to find the beautiful, we must carry it with us, or we find it not.

"When I gaze at the star-sown heaven,
and the infinite beauty it affords my eyes,
that means to me more than all that human art can give me."

~ Mahatma Gandhi
All Men Are Brothers

43

Daily Bread

I enjoy all the hours of life. Few persons have such susceptibility to pleasure; as a countryman will say, "I was at sea a month and never missed a meal," so I eat my dinner and sow my turnips, yet do I never, I think, fear death. It seems to me so often a relief, a rendering-up of responsibility, a quittance of so many vexatious trifles.

It is greatest to believe and to hope well of the world, because the one who does so, quits the world of experience, and makes the world they live in.

The sky is the daily bread of the eyes. What sculpture in these hard clouds; what expression of immense amplitude in this dotted and rippled rack, here firm and continental, there vanishing into plumes and auroral gleams. No crowding; boundless, cheerful, and strong.

"Give us each day our daily bread."

~ Jesus of Nazareth
Gospel of Luke

44

Waiting for a Poet

For it is not metres, but a metre-making argument that makes a poem — a thought so passionate and alive that like the spirit of a plant or an animal it has an architecture of its own, and adorns nature with a new thing. The thought and the form are equal in the order of time, but in the order of genesis the thought is prior to the form. The poet has a new thought; he has a whole new experience to unfold; he will tell us how it was with him, and all men will be the richer in his fortune. For the experience of each new age requires a new confession, and the world seems always waiting for its poet. . . .

We know that the secret of the world is profound, but who or what shall be our interpreter, we know not. A mountain ramble, a new style of face, a new person, may put the key into our hands. Of course the value of genius to us is in the veracity of its report. Talent may frolic and juggle; genius realizes and adds. Mankind in good earnest have availed so far in understanding themselves and their work, that the foremost watchman on the peak announces his news. It is the truest word ever spoken, and the phrase will be the fittest, most musical, and the unerring voice of the world for that time.

"I am a bending aged tree,
That long has stood the wind and rain;
But now has come a cruel blast,
And my last hald of earth is gane."

~ Robert Burns
"Lament for James"

45

Toys

But never can any advantage be taken of nature by
a trick. The spirit of the world, the great calm
presence of the Creator, comes not forth to the sor-
ceries of opium or of wine. The sublime vision
comes to the pure and simple soul in a clean and
chaste body. This is not an inspiration, which we
owe to narcotics, but some counterfeit excitement
and fury. Milton says that the lyric poet may drink
wine and live generously, but the epic poet, he who
shall sing of the gods and their descent unto men,
must drink water out of a wooden bowl. For poetry
is not "Devil's wine," but God's wine. It is with this
as it is with toys. We fill the hands and nurseries of
our children with all manner of dolls, drums and
horses; withdrawing their eyes from the plain face
and sufficing objects of nature, the sun and moon,
the animals, the water and stones, which should be
their toys. So the poet's habit of living should be set
on a key so low that the common influences should
delight him. His cheerfulness should be the gift of
the sunlight; the air should suffice for his inspiration, and he should be tipsy with water. That spirit
which suffices quiet hearts, which seems to come
forth to such from every dry knoll of sere grass,
from every pine stump and half-imbedded stone on

which the dull March sun shines, comes forth to the poor and hungry, and such as are of simple taste. If thou fill thy brain with Boston and New York, with fashion and covetousness, and wilt stimulate thy jaded senses with wine and French coffee, thou shalt find no radiance of wisdom in the lonely waste of the pine woods.

"A lifetime is a child playing a game."

~ Heraclitus
in *Early Greek Philosophy*

46

Gates of the Forest

There are days which occur in this climate, at almost any season of the year, wherein the world reaches its perfection; when the air, the heavenly bodies and the earth, make a harmony, as if nature would indulge her offspring;. . . The day, immeasurably long, sleeps over the broad hills and warm wide fields. To have lived through all its sunny hours, seems longevity enough. The solitary places do not seem quite lonely. At the gates of the forest, the surprised man of the world is forced to leave his city estimates of great and small, wise and foolish. The knapsack of custom falls off his back with the first step he takes into these precincts. Here is sanctity which shames our religions, and reality which discredits our heroes. . . . The stems of pines, hemlocks and oaks almost gleam like iron on the excited eye. The incommunicable trees begin to persuade us to live with them, and quit our life of solemn trifles. Here no history, or church, or state, is interpolated on the divine sky and the immortal year. How easily we might walk onward into the opening landscape, absorbed by new pictures and by thoughts fast succeeding each other, until by degrees the recollection of home was crowded out of the mind, all memory obliterated by the tyranny of the present, and we were led in triumph by nature.

"Welcome are all earth's lands, each for its kind,
Welcome are lands of pine and oak."

~ Walt Whitman
"Song of the Broad-Axe"

47

To Nestle in Nature

Cities give not the human senses room enough. We go out daily and nightly to feed the eyes on the horizon, and require so much scope, just as we need water for our bath. There are all degrees of natural influence, from these quarantine powers of nature, up to her dearest and gravest ministrations to the imagination and the soul. There is the bucket of cold water from the spring, the wood-fire to which the chilled traveller rushes for safety — and there is the sublime moral of autumn and of noon. We nestle in nature, and draw our living as parasites from her roots and grains, and we receive glances from the heavenly bodies, which call us to solitude and foretell the remotest future.

"Wild air, world-mothering air,
Nestling me everywhere."

~ Gerard Manley Hopkins
"The Blessed Virgin compared to the Air we Breathe"

48

The Most Ancient Religion

The fall of snowflakes in a still air, preserving to each crystal its perfect form; the blowing of sleet over a wide sheet of water, and over plains; the waving rye-field; the mimic waving of acres of houstonia, whose innumerable florets whiten and ripple before the eye; the reflections of trees and flowers in glassy lakes; the musical, steaming, odorous south wind, which converts all trees to wind-harps; the crackling and spurting of hemlock in the flames, or of pine, logs, which yield glory to the walls and faces in the sitting-room—these are the music and pictures of the most ancient religion. . . . We penetrate bodily this incredible beauty; we dip our hands in this painted element; our eyes are bathed in these lights and forms. . . . I am taught the poorness of our invention, the ugliness of towns and palaces. Art and luxury have early learned that they must work as enhancement and sequel to this original beauty. I am over-instructed for my return. Henceforth I shall be hard to please. I cannot go back to toys.

"Human beings are religious creatures because they are imaginative; they are so constituted that they are compelled to search for hidden meaning and to achieve an ecstasy that makes them feel fully alive."

~ Karen Armstrong
Islam: A Short History

49

Beauty Breaks in Everywhere

The moral sensibility which makes Edens and Tempes so easily, may not be always found, but the material landscape is never far off. We can find these enchantments without visiting the Como Lake, or the Madeira Islands. We exaggerate the praises of local scenery. In every landscape the point of astonishment is the meeting of the sky and the earth, and that is seen from the first hillock as well as from the top of the Alleghanies. The stars at night stoop down over the brownest, homeliest common with all the spiritual magnificence which they shed on the Campagna, or on the marble deserts of Egypt. The uprolled clouds and the colors of morning and evening will transfigure maples and alders. The difference between landscape and landscape is small, but there is great difference in the beholders. There is nothing so wonderful in any particular landscape as the necessity of being beautiful under which every landscape lies. Nature cannot be surprised in undress. Beauty breaks in everywhere.

"The poet is not just mere clay, or dust returning to dust,
but rather illumination of the light of the heart
breathed into the heart of nature."

~ Nahid Angha
Ecstasy

50

The City of God

Nature is loved by what is best in us. It is loved as the city of God, although, or rather because there is no citizen. The sunset is unlike anything that is underneath it: it wants men. And the beauty of nature must always seem unreal and mocking, until the landscape has human figures that are as good as itself. If there were good men, there would never be this rapture in nature. If the king is in the palace, nobody looks at the walls. It is when he is gone, and the house is filled with grooms and gazers, that we turn from the people to find relief in the majestic men that are suggested by the pictures and the architecture. The critics who complain of the sickly separation of the beauty of nature from the thing to be done, must consider that our hunting of the picturesque is inseparable from our protest against false society. Man is fallen; nature is erect, and serves as a differential thermometer, detecting the presence or absence of the divine sentiment in man. By fault of our dullness and selfishness we are looking up to nature, but when we are convalescent, nature will look up to us. We see the foaming brook with compunction: if our own life flowed with the right energy, we should shame the brook.

*"You are no longer strangers and sojourners,
but you are fellow citizens with the saints
and members of the household of God."*

~ Saul of Tarsus
Letter to the Ephesians

51

Proteus

Let us not longer omit our homage to the Efficient Nature, *natura naturans*, the quick cause before which all forms flee as the driven snows; itself secret, its works driven before it in flocks and multitudes (as the ancients represented nature by Proteus, a shepherd) and in undescribable variety. It publishes itself in creatures, reaching from particles and spiculae through transformation on transformation to the highest symmetries, arriving at consummate results without a shock or a leap. A little heat, that is a little motion, is all that differences the bald, dazzling white and deadly cold poles of the earth from the prolific tropical climates. All changes pass without violence, by reason of the two cardinal conditions of boundless space and boundless time. . . .
It is a long way from granite to the oyster; farther yet to Plato and the preaching of the immortality of the soul. Yet all must come, as surely as the first atom has two sides.

"We balance on a ray of light and an oxygen molecule."

~ Bernd Heinrich
The Trees in My Forest

52

The Young of the World

Nature is always consistent, though she feigns to contravene her own laws. She keeps her laws, and seems to transcend them. She arms and equips an animal to find its place and living in the earth, and at the same time she arms and equips another animal to destroy it. Space exists to divide creatures; but by clothing the sides of a bird with a few feathers she gives him a petty omnipresence. The direction is forever onward, but the artist still goes back for materials and begins again with the first elements on the most advanced stage: otherwise all goes to ruin. If we look at her work, we seem to catch a glance of a system in transition. Plants are the young of the world, vessels of health and vigor; but they grope ever upward towards consciousness; the trees are imperfect men, and seem to bemoan their imprisonment, rooted in the ground. The animal is the novice and probationer of a more advanced order. The men, though young, having tasted the first drop from the cup of thought, are already dissipated; the maples and ferns are still uncorrupt; yet no doubt when they come to consciousness they too will curse and swear. Flowers so strictly belong to youth that we adults soon come to feel that their beautiful generations concern not us: we have had our day; now let the children have theirs. The flowers jilt us, and we are old bachelors with our ridiculous tenderness.

"We have made our mark on the world, but we have really done nothing that the trees and creeping plants, ice and erosion, cannot remove in a fairly short time."

~ John Steinbeck
The Log from the Sea of Cortez

53

Encamped in Nature

We are encamped in nature, not domesticated. Hunger and thirst lead us on to eat and to drink; but bread and wine, mix and cook them how you will, leave us hungry and thirsty, after the stomach is full. It is the same with all our arts and performances. Our music, our poetry, our language itself are not satisfactions, but suggestions. The hunger for wealth, which reduces the planet to a garden, fools the eager pursuer. What is the end sought? Plainly to secure the ends of good sense and beauty from the intrusion of deformity or vulgarity of any kind. But what an operose method! What a train of means to secure a little conversation! This palace of brick and stone, these servants, this kitchen, these stables, horses and equipage, this bank-stock and file of mortgages; trade to all the world, country-house and cottage by the waterside, all for a little conversation, high, clear and spiritual! Could it not be had as well by beggars on the highway?

"A fine place for feasting if only one be poor enough."

~ John Muir
"Mountain Thoughts" in *The Journals*

54

Not Near Enough

There is in woods and waters a certain enticement and flatter, together with a failure to yield a present satisfaction. This disappointment is felt in every landscape. I have seen the softness and beauty of the summer clouds floating feathery overhead, enjoying, as it seemed, their height and privilege of motion, whilst yet they appeared not so much the drapery of this place and hour, as forelooking to some pavilions and gardens of festivity beyond. It is an odd jealousy, but the poet finds himself not near enough to his object. The pine-tree, the river, the bank of flowers before him does not seem to be nature. Nature is still elsewhere. This or this is but outskirt and a far-off reflection and echo of the triumph that has passed by and is now at its glancing splendor and heyday, perchance in the neighboring fields, or, if you stand in the field, then in the adjacent woods. The present object shall give you this sense of stillness that follows a pageant which has just gone by. What splendid distance, what recesses of ineffable pomp and loveliness in the sunset! But who can go where they are, or lay his hand or plant his foot thereon? Off they fall from the round world forever and ever. It is the same among the men and women as among the silent trees; always a referred existence, an absence, never a presence and satisfaction. Is it that beauty can never be grasped?

"If you are confused, mountains and rivers block your way."

~ Sandokai
Harmony of Difference and Sameness (Zen service)

55

Tickled Trout

Are we tickled trout, and fools of nature? One look at the face of heaven and earth lays all petulance at rest, and soothes us to wiser convictions. To the intelligent, nature converts itself into a vast promise, and will not be rashly explained. Her secret is untold. Many and many an Oedipus arrives; he has the whole mystery teeming in his brain. Alas! the same sorcery has spoiled his skill; no syllable can he shape on his lips. Her mighty orbit vaults like the fresh rainbow into the deep, but no archangel's wing was yet strong enough to follow it and report of the return of the curve. But it also appears that our actions are seconded and disposed to greater conclusions than we designed. We are escorted on every hand through life by spiritual agents, and a beneficent purpose lies in wait for us.

*"And We send down from the sky Rain
Charged with blessing."*

~ The Qur'an
Surah Fifty

56

A Present Sanity

After every foolish day we sleep off the fumes and furies of its hours; and though we are always engaged with particulars, and often enslaved to them, we bring with us to every experiment the innate universal laws. These, while they exist in the mind as ideas, stand around us in nature forever embodied, a present sanity to expose and cure the insanity of men. Our servitude to particulars betrays us into a hundred foolish expectations. We anticipate a new era from the invention of a locomotive, or a balloon; the new engine brings with it the old checks. They say that by electro-magnetism your salad shall be grown from the seed whilst your fowl is roasting for dinner; it is a symbol of our modern aims and endeavors, of our condensation and acceleration of objects; but nothing is gained; nature cannot be cheated; man's life is but seventy salads long, grow they swift or grow they slow. . . . That power which does not respect quantity, which makes the whole and the particle its equal channel, delegates its smile to the morning, and distils its essence into every drop of rain. Every moment instructs, and every object; for wisdom is infused into every form.

"A bodhisattva's spiritual practices
act as wings to enlightenment."

~ The Buddha
The Large Sutra on Perfect Wisdom

57

Save the Present Moment

I go twice a week over Concord with Ellery [Channing], and, as we sit on the steep park at Conantum, we still have the same regret as oft before. Is all this beauty to perish? Shall none remake this sun and wind, the sky-blue river, the river-blue sky; the yellow meadow spotted with sacks and sheets of cranberry-pickers; the red bushes; the iron-gray house with just the color of the granite rock; the paths of the thicket, in which the only engineers are the cattle grazing on yonder hill; the wide, straggling wild orchard in which Nature has deposited every possible flavor in the apples of different trees? Whole zones and climates she has concentrated into apples. We think of the old benefactors who have conquered these fields; of the old man Moore, who is just dying in these days, who has absorbed such volumes of sunshine like a huge melon or pumpkin in the sun,—who has owned in every part of Concord a woodlot, until he could not find the boundaries of these, and never saw their interiors. But we say, where is the one who is to save the present moment, and cause that this beauty be not lost?

"When I look at the earth
in pictures taken from space
I see no boundaries
no boundaries
no border patrols
no sign of ownership
of the land or the seas
or the mountains
or the lakes
or the rivers
I feel like a planetary citizen."

~ Shurli Grant
"Planetary Citizens," in *Rainbow*

58

Sweeter Rivers Silent

Thy voice is sweet, Musketaquid; repeats the music of the rain; but sweeter rivers silent flit through thee, as thou through Concord plain.

Thou art shut in thy banks; but the stream I love, flows in thy water, and flows through rocks and through the air, and through darkness, and through men, and women. I hear and see the inundation and eternal spending of the stream, in winter and in summer, in men and animals, in passion and thought. Happy are they who can hear it.

I see thy brimming, eddying stream, and thy enchantment. For thou changest every rock in thy bed into a gem: all is real opal and agate, and at will thou pavest with diamonds. Take them away from thy stream, and they are poor shards and flints: so is it with me today.

*"We remembered what we had forgotten:
that immense spirits precede us—always—
when we travel on rivers."*

~ Rebecca Lawton
Reading Water

59

Deep Green Leaves

Sources of Inspiration. Solitary converse with Nature is. . .perhaps the first, and there are ejaculated sweet and dreadful words never uttered in libraries. Ah, the spring days, summer dawns, and October woods!

How shallow seemed to me yesterday in the woods the speech one often hears from tired citizens who have spent their brief enthusiasm for the country, that Nature is tedious, and they have had enough of green leaves. Nature and the green leaves are a million fathoms deep, and it is these eyes that are superficial.

When I bought my farm, I did not know what a bargain I had in the bluebirds, bobolinks, and thrushes; as little did I know what sublime mornings and sunsets I was buying.

"And
the old woman said
I am earth
tell them
that I love them."

~ Malcolm Jones
"Earth," in *The Sacraments Flame*

60

I Am Still at Home

Self-sown my stately garden grows;
The winds and wind-blown seed,
Cold April rain and colder snows
My hedges plant and feed.

From mountains far and valleys near
The harvests sown today
Thrive in all weathers without fear,
Wild planters, plant away!

In cities high the careful crowds
Of woe-worn mortals darkling go,
But in these sunny solitudes
My quiet roses blow.

Methought the sky looked scornful down
On all was base in man,
And airy tongues did taunt the town,
"Achieve our peace who can!"

The air is wise, the wind thinks well,
And all through which it blows,
If plants or brain, if egg or shell,
Or bird or biped knows;

And oft at home 'mid tasks I heed,
I heed how wears the day;
We must not halt while fiercely speed
The spans of life away.

What boots it here of Thebes or Rome
Or lands of Eastern day?
In forests I am still at home
And there I cannot stray.

"We must also care for our environment.
This is our home, our only home!"

~ The Dalai Lama
An Open Heart

Afterword

Good-Bye

Good-bye, proud world! I'm going home:
Thou art not my friend, and I'm not thine.
Long through thy weary crowds I roam;
A river-ark on the ocean brine,
Long I've been tossed like the driven foam;
But now, proud world! I'm going home.

I am going to my own hearth-stone,
Bosomed in yon green hills alone—
A secret nook in a pleasant land,
Whose groves the frolic fairies planned;
Where arches green, the livelong day,
Echo the blackbird's roundelay,
And vulgar feet have never trod
A spot that is sacred to thought and God.

O, when I am safe in my sylvan home,
I tread on the pride of Greece and Rome;
And when I am stretched beneath the pines,
Where the evening star so holy shines,
I laugh at the lore and the pride of man,
At the sophist schools and the learned clan;
For what are they all, in their high conceit,
When man in the bush with God may meet?

~ Ralph Waldo Emerson
from "Good-Bye"

Sources

In the preceding text the source of each Emerson quote is identified by a particular leaf icon, shown following the passage. Below is a key to those sources:

An Address (1838)

American Scholar (1837)

Art (1841)

Circles (1841)

Friendship (1841)

Journals: July 13, 1833 *(quote 1)*
April 11, 1834 *(quote 2)*
September 15, 1834 *(quote 3)*
February 28, 1836 *(quote 4)*
November 6, 1837 *(quote 12)*
April 26, 1838 *(quote 17)*

Nature (1844)

Spiritual Laws (1841)

Walden (poem)

*The Complete Essays and Other Writings of
Ralph Waldo Emerson*
> Edited by Brooks Atkinson.
> N.Y.: Random House, 1950.

The Heart of Emerson's Journals
> Edited by Bliss Perry.
> N.Y.: Dover Publications, 1995. Reprint of
> the 1926 Houghton Mifflin edition.

Emerson: The Mind on Fire
> Robert Richardson, Jr.
> Berkeley: University of California Press,
> 1995.

*My Heart is a Large Kingdom:
Selected Letters of Margaret Fuller*
> Margaret Fuller,
> Edited by Robert N. Hudspeth.
> Ithaca, N.Y.: Cornell University Press,
> 2001.

Selections from Ralph Waldo Emerson
> Edited by Stephen E. Whicher.
> Boston: Houghton Mifflin, 1957.

Meditations of Ralph Waldo Emerson: Into the Green Future was created on a Power Macintosh G3, using QuarkXPress 4.1 and Adobe Photoshop 5.5. The text and display font is Bitstream's *Calligraphic 810*; the "leaf" icons belong to Andrew D. Taylor's *ArborisFolium*; and the "book" and "oak leaf" graphics belong to P22's *Arts and Crafts Ornaments 2*.

Photo Credits

*C*hris Highland is an interspiritual chaplain, author, songwriter and poet. He completed his undergraduate studies in religion and philosophy in Seattle, Washington before settling in the San Francisco Bay Area to complete his Masters degree. A passionate saunterer, he enjoys an intimate relation with Nature in forests, mountains and waterfalls. An avowed heretic ("one who seeks new paths"), Chris's writing reflects his exploration of the edges of human society and his playful search for what Emerson called "high, clear and spiritual conversation," to be had by each and every one of us as "beggars on the highway."

Chris is the author of *Meditations of John Muir: Nature's Temple* and *Meditations of Henry David Thoreau: A Light in the Woods*, both from Wilderness Press. An eclectic map of Chris's creative thought and colorful photography can be read and seen at www.naturetemple.net.

More meditations ...

Meditations of
John Muir:
Nature's Temple

Insightful quotations from America's preeminent naturalist, writer, and activist are paired with selections from other celebrated thinkers and spiritual texts.

ISBN 0-89997-285-3

Meditations of
Henry David Thoreau:
A Light in the Woods

A sampler of 60 thoughtful quotations from America's first great conservationist and preeminent social critic, paired with reflections from other spiritual traditions..

ISBN 0-89997-321-3

Meditations of
Walt Whitman:
Earth, My Likeness

Contains 60 passages from Whitman's great planting of poems, Leaves of Grass, *compiled over a lifetime spanning nearly the entire 19th century, plus complementary quotes from others.*

ISBN 0-89997-362-0

CPSIA information can be obtained at www.ICGtesting.com
Printed in the USA
LVOW01n2027060515

437435LV00003B/8/P